SECRETS *of the* LEVELS

SECRETS *of the* LEVELS

CHRIS CHAPMAN

Somerset Books

in association with HTV Limited

First Published in Great Britain in 1996 by Somerset Books

The poem on page 55, 'Another Early Morning: circa 1520 AD'
is reproduced by kind permission of James Crowden

British Library Cataloguing in Publication Data

Data for this publication is available from the British Library

ISBN 0 86183 308 2

SOMERSET BOOKS
Official Publisher to Somerset County Council

Halsgrove House
Lower Moor Way
Tiverton EX16 6SS
Tel: 01884 243242
Fax: 01884 243325

Reprographics by Peninsular Repro Services, Exeter
Printed and bound in Great Britain by Hillman Printers (Frome) Ltd

Contents

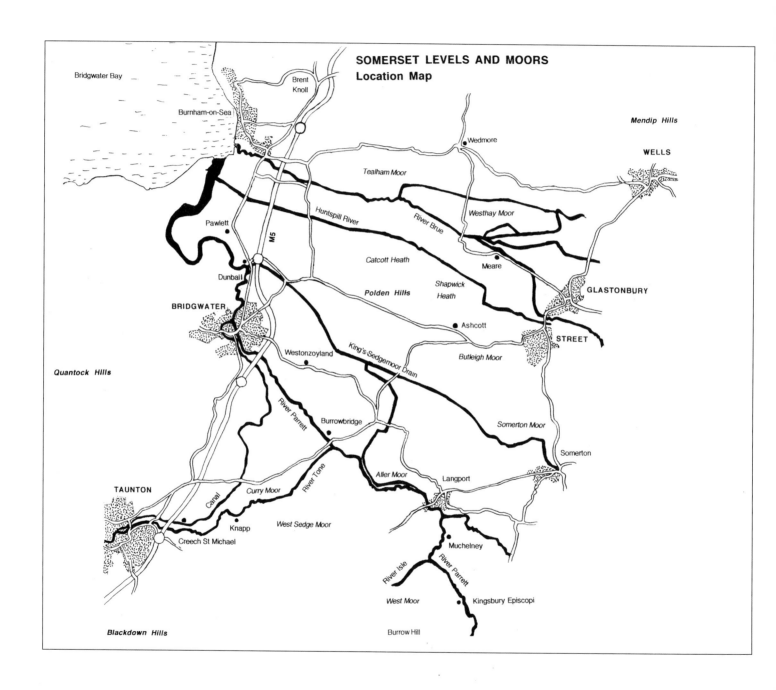

SOMERSET LEVELS AND MOORS
Location Map

Foreword
by Chris Chapman

If you travel down country on the London to Penzance line and the time of the year is winter, the train suddenly emerges from the hills into a land of water and sky. The glimpse is brief but the senses record an extraordinary scene. Above you the sky is teeming with birdlife, and the watery meadows, now flat and distant, are broken only by the stumps of trees, their crowns bursting with a head of spiky hair.

People have told me that their spirit was lifted by this scene and then all too soon the train pulled into Taunton and the magic was gone.

This may have been your only taste of the land we now call the Somerset Levels and, if this is so, I hope to introduce you to a fascinating landscape. I have been in love with this area for many years and although I have often heard it described as flat and uninteresting believe me the opposite is true.

The walks that I have outlined have been explored with variety in mind, so that each has something new to offer whilst illustrating the uniqueness of the area. I hope you enjoy them and like me grow to love the place. If you do then this book will have served its purpose well.

Although they are in need of updating, Ordnance Survey maps of the 'Pathfinder' series are essential for the walks. The scale of $2^{1}/_{2}$ inches to the mile (4cm to the kilometre if you are a metric baby) gives excellent detail and will help you to read the landscape. The relevant sheet numbers as well as an approximate mileage are given at the start of each walk.

Rules for walking are a pain, but I would ask you to try and remember this: all land belongs to somebody. Farm gates need closing behind you, dogs should be on a lead if they have a taste for lamb and duck, and there is nothing more unpleasant than coming across the debris of someone else's picnic. Leave no trace of your passing and hopefully others will do the same. As regards footwear, the time of year will dictate. I prefer leather boots and gaiters but in winter the ground is sodden and you may prefer wellingtons. The soil cloys, however, and you will definitely slide about!

May I also suggest the following books to add to your library. *The Natural History of the Somerset Levels* by Bernard Storer is an excellent work that manages to be scientific yet immensely readable. Robin Bush's *Somerset: The Complete Guide* gives a fascinating background to the villages and towns and *Wetland*, by Adam Nicholson with the photographer Patrick Sutherland, is a charming portrait of life in the Levels caught in the mid-1980s.

for Helen

Introduction

On a cold autumn morning, when the mist hangs over the meadows and the willows melt into the distance, the Somerset Levels appear as an ancient land. The atmosphere of the place certainly is, but much of the visual presence is surprisingly recent. A little of the geographical and historical background illustrates why.

10,500 years ago the glaciers that had gripped the Northern Hemisphere intermittently throughout the Ice Age were on their final retreat. The surrounding hills of the Mendips, Poldens, Blackdowns and Quantocks were now shaping into their present form, their broad valley bottoms coursing rivers to a distant and icy sea.

Patches of woodland and shrub had developed on these valley floors but by 7000 BC the ice cap had melted and the sea began to rise.

Some two thousand years later the climate had reached its warmest. A shallow sea now covered the area, building muddy clays on the sea bed. In turn the rivers, moving at a much slower pace, deposited soils washed down from the hills. A small drop in sea level then exposed this mud to the air.

By 4000 BC the colonisation of the area by plant life was well under way. Near to the sea a belt of silt and clay formed, raising itself slightly higher than the land behind. Although not truly landlocked (the rivers still found their way to the sea), the area flooded with fresh water with the sea encroaching in times of storm and high tide. These were now the right conditions for the creation of pool and marsh. Reed and sedge grew and rotted, the debris compacting to form peat and firming the land for the invasion of other plants.

An erratic climatic pattern throughout the following centuries saw the landscape change many times with areas of swamp, fenwood or raised bog prevailing.

Throughout all this, mankind's grip on Sedgemoor was a gradual process. Cave dwellers and later Mesolithic peoples would have had little impact on the land, their lifestyle dependent on hunting, fishing and gathering food.

It was the Neolithic culture, spreading from the Mediterranean, that introduced the practice of farming and altered the scene. These people populated not only the hill slopes, but now planted cereal crops and pastured their animals, moving across the peat bogs by means of sophisticated wooden trackways. They knew the art of coppicing and, for the first time in its history, the wildwood of hill and heath was cleared and managed by man.

Their effect on the lowlands, however, was minimal. They would, of course, have taken advantage of everything Sedgemoor had to offer. The warmer summers allowed for some pasture and in the winter the flooded areas were a rich resource of fish and wildlife.

This pattern continued throughout the Bronze and Iron Ages, though now attempts at settling on the marshland itself are in evidence in the 'lake villages' found to the north of the Poldens, at Meare and Glastonbury. (Though it has to be argued that these tribal settlements were probably on better drained land.)

The coming of the Romans brought new ideas. There is plenty of evidence for Romano British settlement on the drier ground and on the raised coastal clay belt. The ridge road along the Poldens linking the Roman ports of Combwich and Crandon Bridge with the Fosseway into Ilchester was an important route. We know of their drainage skills from those implemented in the eastern Fens and although there is no proof, it is possible that they built the first sea defences and drained the marsh by the coast.

There is evidence of saltings where the Romans extracted sea salt near to the village of Burtle and also a large number of pottery sites. Around 250 AD the sea encroached over a large area depositing a thick layer of clay and silt. One wonders if these finds indicate later activity, driven further inland by the flooding.

If the Romans did drain larger areas then the evidence now lies under the soil. By the time they left in the fifth century their administration had collapsed and we enter an age of decay. As the Angles, Saxons and Jutes swept into the country, first on plundering raids and later to settle, the pages of history go blank and we wait for archaeology to help unravel the tale.

By the seventh century a picture emerges of a well structured Saxon kingdom and a heathen society converting to Christianity, later suffering the plundering raids of the Vikings. The defeat of Guthrum, his baptism at Aller and the signing of a peace treaty with Alfred at Wedmore in 878 is a colourful piece of history. It also tell us of a Sedgemoor as yet untamed.

But the scene was set to alter. The dawn of monastic power brought radical change to the Levels. By the time of the Norman conquest, the religious houses were well established and throughout the following centuries more and more land was brought into agricultural use. Sedgemoor was harnessed though not conquered. The rivers were damned for fisheries, walls were built to prevent flooding, both on the coast and around sections of moor, and drainage channels were dug in an attempt to divert the rivers and control the water.

Their efforts, though skilled, showed little consideration for Sedgemoor as a whole. The greed for land caused many a dispute between abbot and bishop with conflicting interests causing one scheme to disrupt another. When Henry VIII curbed monastic power in 1538 the drive to reclaim the land began to dwindle. A drainage scheme put forward in the time of King James I when he laid claim to what is now King's Sedgemoor came to nothing due to a lack of co-ordination with the surrounding landowners. This pattern seemed set to continue and little was implemented or achieved. Flooding remained a fact of life.

From time out of mind the Levels had also been the domain of the commoner and peasant. Content with the minimum of reclamation, he pastured his cattle in summer, grazed huge flocks of geese for their meat and feathers and reaped whatever the Levels would give or grow. For him there was no great interest in enclosure for that brought a loss of rights.

But it was the enclosure Acts of the late eighteenth century and the fever for agricultural improvement that gave us the land-scape we see today. The commoner was now displaced. Between 1770 and 1833 the moors were reclaimed on a grand scale by a system of ditches, rhynes and drains. Willow was planted to strengthen the banks, and meadow and pasture created. The invention of the steam engine in the nineteenth century and its use as a pump also gave the landowners a means of clearing the flood waters and for the first time in its history the Levels were close to being tamed.

So the landscape we see today represents centuries of endeavour turning land that was once wild into agricultural use. It is a modern scene that has now reached a crossroads. Everyone wishes to see a balance between nature and agriculture and we are acutely aware of the dangers of technology: it is capable of destroying the very heart of the place.

With the fragility of Sedgemoor in mind a compromise has been reached which, for now, seems fair. The farmers are held back from improvement and asked to farm with conservation in mind and the Government, recognising their frustration, pays with a system of compensation. Heads continue to bang together but it is still a considerable achievement.

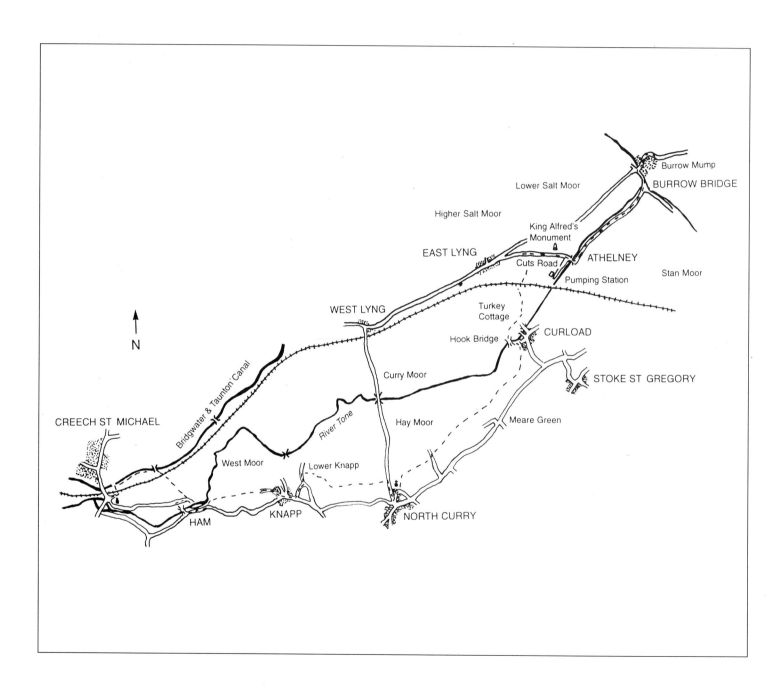

Burrow Mump

Lower Salt Moor

BURROW BRIDGE

Higher Salt Moor

King Alfred's
Monument

Stan Moor

EAST LYNG

Cuts Road

ATHELNEY

Pumping Station

WEST LYNG

Turkey
Cottage

CURLOAD

Hook Bridge

STOKE ST GREGORY

N

Curry Moor

Bridgwater & Taunton Canal

River Tone

Hay Moor

Meare Green

CREECH ST MICHAEL

West Moor

Lower Knapp

HAM

KNAPP

NORTH CURRY

Withy Heartland and the Valley of the Tone:

CREECH ST MICHAEL, HAM MILLS, KNAPP, NORTH CURRY, CURLOAD, ATHELNEY, BURROW MUMP

(Pathfinder map 1258) 8½ miles.

Creech St Michael is a parish too close to Taunton, for in recent years it has become a dormitory for the town, expanding rapidly with modern homes. Starting the walk here, though, has an advantage for you experience the contrast of urban and rural within a few short paces.

Before leaving the village visit the church of St Michael. Built high above the river, it has developed in an unusual form with the bell tower placed awkwardly in the north elevation. There is much to see inside, including a Georgian minstrels' gallery, and outside in the graveyard stand ancient yew trees and the old village stocks. Carved initials laid into the perimeter wall identify parishioners who paid for each section in return for grazing on local common land.

Park in the canal car park at Creech St Michael and join the towpath of the Bridgwater and Taunton Canal.

Unfortunately this stretch is a depository for rubbish and dog walk alley (every village has one), but it doesn't last long, and I doubt at this stage you will be needing the 'Rest A While' bench. On reaching the first bridge (No. 17 Foxhole), leave the canal path and go past Cathill Farm towards the London to Penzance railway track. STOP, LOOK AND LISTEN is obviously sound advice but before crossing the line cast your eyes around.

You may have thought that recycling was a late twentieth century invention but here the kissing gate has been fashioned out of the old broad gauge track and the lengthman's hut nearby is built with wooden sleepers.

Follow the footpath across the fields and cross the Tone by the footbridge just above the weir. You are now in the hamlet of Ham. Turn left and walk along the lane until you reach the suspension bridge over the river at Ham Mills.

This is a beautiful spot with an interesting history. Although we think of Bridgwater as the port, there are records to show that the Tone was being used for navigation to Taunton as early as the fifteenth century for the trading of fuel, grain and wine and at one time would have been quite busy. The weir below Ham bridge, necessary to control water to the mill, hindered progress up the river and caused disputes between the Dean and Chapter of Wells (who held North Curry) and the Bishop of Winchester who lorded over Taunton Deane. The building on the island was a millhouse and amid the ruins and undergrowth are the remains of the last mill with its waterwheel still intact.

On the other side of the river via the suspension bridge is Coal Harbour although on the map it is marked as the Rookery. When names change the clues to the area's history disappear.

1

Work carried out on the river-banks in the 1960s revealed an old ford spanning the river bed. Horse and cart would have crossed here to fetch coal that had been shipped up the Tone.

The private bridge was designed and built by Royal Marine Engineers in 1968, replacing a bridge further downstream.

From Ham Mills take the footpath on your right across the fields and up the hill to Knapp. At the top, the footpath has been diverted as recently as September 1995, taking you through the orchard of Birds Farm and not on the track. Walk down the lane and into the hamlet of Knapp. As you walk along the ridge towards Higher Knapp Farm you will pass a chimney on your left, built of brick and looking a little out of place. This is a withy boiler and the Derham brothers who run it incorporate the withy trade into their farming activity.

Osiers, or withies as they are more commonly known, have probably been harvested on Sedgemoor from time out of mind. The willow loves damp conditions and its straight yet bendable branches have great strength, making it suitable for all types of domestic use. It was woven into baskets, was used for fish traps and hurdles for animals and as a building material for houses.

In the nineteenth century the osiers were planted on a commercial scale and the wild stock improved. This led to a boom in the industry supplying everything from baskets and cradles to garden furniture. It was the perfect crop and could withstand periods under water in times of flood.

To establish a new withy bed green willow cuttings about eight inches in length are planted out in neat rows in the spring and by autumn will have reached a height of over 6 feet. After the leaves have dropped and before the sap can rise again, the plants are cut back to a stump. These in turn will sprout again with a number of shoots and the following winter the first harvest is cropped. A bed like this can last for up to fifty years.

After cutting, the withies are sorted and bundled. Brown withies (with the bark left on) are simply air dried and stored. To produce white willows, bundles of cut withies are stood in a pond in about a foot of water and left there until May. By then they will have rooted and sprung into leaf making the bark easy to strip and revealing the white wood. If it is left later than this another skin forms underneath and the bark will not come off.

To produce the buff colour the process is more labour intensive. Stan Derham explains the procedure.

> To get the buff colour we have to boil the withies for seven hours solid. The tank'll take about 140 wads of willows. Once we've started it's a job we've got to keep going with because every minute that the boiler is open we are losing steam and heat. We keep feeding her with coal and we've got to keep pressing them down until we've finished loading and then we put bars across them to keep them in. They've got to be kept underneath water all the time because if they don't they burn.

The withies are then fed into a brake, a mechanical rotating drum which strips the bark. Before the 1930s this was always done by hand by the women and children of the surrounding villages. It was very tedious work as the willows had to be pulled through a V-shaped metal tool, one at a time. The stripped willows are then spread out onto wires to dry and then graded and bundled ready for the basket maker.

All this activity makes for an industry that is very labour intensive and no one yet has invented a machine that can make a basket. The costs of production are high but, as Stanley points out, the future for the industry looks bright:

> It was pretty good here during the war, and then afterwards when the plastic came in it knocked the willows right out. A lot of willow people went out of business and it slowed up. Now people are going back to more natural things.

The Derham brothers with their withy boiler, Knapp.

Stanley Derham on the withy beds, West Moor, Knapp.
'Some day this will all be sea again, but not in my lifetime.'

Reggie Hector, with Geoff and Mark Pipe, cutting withies on West Sedgemoor.

Geoff Pipe loading withies, North Curry.

Reggie Hector and Geoff Pipe loading their crop into a pit, Stoke St Gregory. In May these will be stripped to produce white withies.

Simon Boobyer stripping willows with a brake, Stathe.

Walk down the hill to Lower Knapp and if you are hungry by now then a good pub lunch can be had at the Rising Sun, which specialises in fish from Brixham and the local smoked eel.

Further on down, take the path to your right across the fields to North Curry which will bring you out onto Moor Lane just below the church. Walk up into the village.

The centre of North Curry has a genteel air that once merged with a working atmosphere. It still has a charming post office and two inns, but the large grocery store has closed succumbing to the loss of customers travelling to the supermarkets of Taunton. It is a sad fact of village life that such shops, once the centre for gossip and bustle, are now on the decline.

A pleasant surprise in the village is the show of topiary at the back of the Regency brick house at the start of Knapp Lane. Yew, bay, laurel and privet have been snipped into simple shapes and planted close together and the end result is a bundle of fun.

Cross over Queen's Square and visit the church of SS Peter and Paul. Its appearance is rather grand and the original fourteenth century steep pitched roof has been raised and embattled. This, and its links with the Dean and Chapter of Wells, have given it the local title of 'the Cathedral of the Moors'.

Leave the church by the north-east gate and walk along the edge of the field and up the steep hill to Moredon. From here to Windmill Hill the views are stunning and the walking easy. In winter the moor is often flooded and teeming with birdlife and in summer a warm breeze sweeps up from the Tone.

'The Cathedral of the Moors', North Curry church.

Chris Mico winding the church clock, North Curry.

'When we had a few years dry the north wall of the church began to subside, but now its back to normal. Flooding used to be a regular routine and we accepted it but farmers now want more out of the ground than nature is prepared to give. I don't mind the flooding. You can't fight nature.'

View from Windmill Hill. The River Tone in flood.

A diversion will take you to the Willows and Wetlands Visitor Centre at Meare Green Court, although I suggest a separate trip by car.

The proprietors, the Coates, employ a number of people to make baskets. When I visited the centre I noticed that one or two baskets for sale stood out from others. They were strong yet very fine. Norman Upham, born in 1913, who made them, used to have his own workshop in the village but now works at the centre:

> When I left school I went butchering but then I came home where my father lived and I started doing outdoor work on the withies. We were making real rough baskets, I reckon that half the parish worked at it, the roughest things you've ever seen. It's what they used to take yeast to Ireland in.
>
> We used to make butchers' carriers, you know, to sit on the bicycles. We knew nearly all the bicycle firms then. And when the war was on we made baskets to drop to the troops. I had my own business in the chapel but when I finished at sixty-five they put my business rates up and I had to give them half my pension every week to keep it open. It got worse and worse and did nearly kill ye off. So I closed it down and they have nothing and I come up here to work for these. I can come up here but I don't work as hard as they do. They work like fly machines. I used to!
>
> I've been making baskets for sixty-two years and I've never had a basket back, never in my life.

Norman Upham with one of his baskets,
P. H. Coate & Son, Meare Green.

Modern withy cutter, P. H. Coate & Son.

From Windmill Hill the path drops down and joins the track over Hook Bridge. Take the path a short way along the drove then follow the raised bank, with Turkey Cottage on your left, and join Crooked Drove to the East Lyng to Athelney road, taking care as you cross back over the railway.

Turkey Cottage and its occupants, the Billingtons, hit national news in the winter of 1994/95 as the floodwaters of the River Tone rose to a new high on Curry Moor. Upstream from Hook Bridge is a spillway, designed to flood Curry Moor when the upper reaches of the Tone threaten Taunton. The Athelney Pumping Station then relieves the moor of its water when conditions allow.

There was some argument that the river had been allowed to silt up but, whatever the cause, days of continuous rainfall in the hills, coupled with high spring tides, meant that the rivers could not cope. There was no point in pumping until low tide and, despite an extra pump being installed at the station, the waters continued to rise.

For the Billingtons this was alarming but not unusual as they had bought their cottage knowing it could flood, and so they moved upstairs and travelled about by boat. Then they lost their heat and power. Forced to leave, it was on their return that they found a level of 34 inches recorded by the dirty brown stain on the living room wall!

As you walk towards Athelney island a clue in the landscape shows that the Billingtons' misfortune can be blamed on the past. Crooked Drove meanders towards the gap between East Lyng and the Isle of Athelney and was at one time the old course of the River Tone. The river then split into two channels, one heading north through the gap to join the Parrett further downstream, and the other heading along the south flank of the island towards the Mump.

North Curry Pumping Station. In the winter of 1994/95 an extra pump was brought in to clear the floodwater.

The Billingtons setting out for their flooded cottage, Curry Moor.

The Middle Ages were a period of monastic fervour, with a great interest in reclaiming land for its agricultural potential. The Isle of Athelney once housed an abbey, and in the fourteenth century the Abbot diverted the river in order to prevent flooding on Salt Moor, digging the present day cut of the Tone and raising its banks. The building of Baltmoor Wall (part of which is now Cuts Road) consolidated these works, plugging the gap and serving as a permanent causeway to the island.

It was a case however of 'I'm alright Jack', for although the scheme protected Salt Moor it caused problems for the Dean and Chapter of Wells on their land at Stathe Moor. The Abbot was severely reprimanded 'for illegally appropriating a water course' and to this day the single outfall of the Tone causes more problems than the scheme solved.

At Cuts Road turn right and walk past Athelney Farm. Behind the tidy farm buildings one can make out the squat shape of a stone monument on the island summit, built in 1801 to commemorate King Alfred.

Cast your mind for a minute and imagine this scene in the ninth century. You are on a boat staring at an island surrounded by marsh. There are blankets of sedge and reed and the drier land holds a tangle of willow and alder. On the southern slope you can just see through to a wooden palisade surrounding a settlement that shelters from the cold winds blowing across the water.

Here King Alfred had his fort and, despite the burning of the cakes, the island proved the perfect hideaway from which to plan his last campaign against the Danes. Alfred defeated King Guthrum in 878 and it is thought that in gratitude he founded the abbey on the island. Recent exploration by the television crew 'Time Team' showed, by the use of geophysics, the footings of a small rectangular building within the later abbey ruins. It is quite likely that this was Alfred's Saxon church. Cross over the bridge at Athelney rather than taking the path along the

river across to Cular Rhyne. The A361 is a fast and busy road and you will find the lane to Burrow Bridge far quieter.

Most of the cottages from Curload to Burrow Bridge are built on the east bank, well above the threat of flooding on the moor but perilously close to the river. The ground is solid here and it says a lot for the monks' skill that the later builders trusted their handiwork! I like the way the river has become the back garden with tame and wild duck making use of the 'pond'.

The lane is an absolute delight, for here is a countryside unfettered by heritage and escaping the eye of the planner. This is a working landscape with no wish to be smart. The vegetables and flowers grow side by side. The local garage serves the car and the tractor, and in orchards old and new the fowl share the grass with the sheep. There is even a bakery.

At the end of the lane turn left and cross over the bridge. Here the Tone meets the Parrett. If you have the energy left it is worth the climb to the top of the Mump. For a long time it was thought to be totally man made, but it is now known to have been raised only at the summit for the purpose of defence, at first by Alfred and later by the Normans.

The church on the top is dedicated to St Michael but is a disappointing edifice that suffered a rebuilding programme in the eighteenth century. Made up of blue lias, ham stone and Bridgwater brick, it was built by subscription but ran out of money and never made it to the roof stage. There are fragments of an earlier chapel within its stonework, notably the gargoyles and faces.

Though the church lacks architectural note, the hill commands some of the best views over Sedgemoor and my favourite is looking west towards Bridgwater. Behind the stilts of the M5, St Mary's spire shoots up like a drawn dagger. The distant hum of traffic and all that that represents make the quieter moors even more attractive.

The Isle of Athelney.

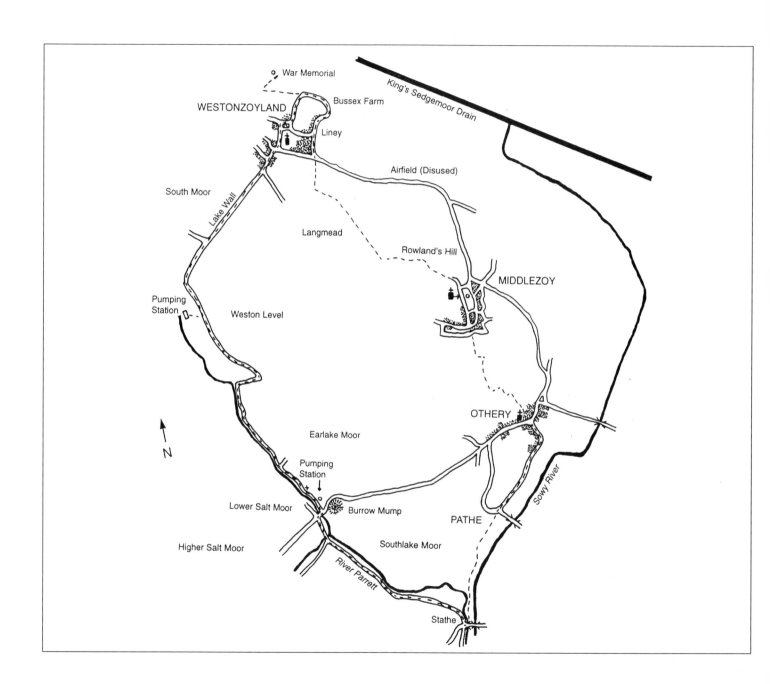

War Memorial

WESTONZOYLAND

Bussex Farm

Liney

Airfield (Disused)

King's Sedgemoor Drain

South Moor

Lake Wall

Langmead

Rowland's Hill

MIDDLEZOY

Pumping Station

Weston Level

N

Earlake Moor

OTHERY

Pumping Station

Lower Salt Moor

Burrow Mump

PATHE

Sowy River

Higher Salt Moor

Southlake Moor

River Parrett

Stathe

The Island Settlements:

BURROW MUMP, WESTONZOYLAND, MIDDLEZOY, OTHERY, STATHE TO BURROW MUMP

(Pathfinder map 1237 & 1258) 12 miles.

This is a circular walk and although some of it is along country lanes, the roads are relatively quiet. I have chosen this walk for a number of reasons. This is the heartland of the Somerset moors and the walk reveals man's endeavours to tame them. It also gives a good insight into the development of the villages on the highest ground.

From Burrow Mump car park, climb up the hill to the skeletal church. From here you can cast your eye over a wide area and imagine King Alfred doing the same. Exhausted from the battles with Guthrum, Alfred went into hiding at Athelney just a mile to the south-west. I like to think he would have stood on this spot, perhaps not to enjoy the views, but to plan his final strike. Hill tops have a way of evoking a feeling of dominance.

Walk down towards the school and through a gate, crossing the busy main road with care. Take the side lane down towards the Parrett. To your left is the bridge that gave the parish its name. Built in 1826 by John Stone of Yarcombe, it has an internal span of some 50 feet or more, and is said to be the longest single span bridge in the county. Note the circular flood relief holes at either end.

Turn right, and immediately to your right is a small track leading to the Allermoor Pumping Station. The name is a little confusing as we are some distance from Allermoor, but the designers utilised the old bed of the River Cary as their main drainage rhyne in order to build the outfall below the confluence of the Tone and Parrett. Completed in 1869, its steam engine proved very effective at clearing flood water. Walter Musgrave, the station's last attendant, told me his story:

I came here in 1934 on a salary of £12 per annum, the house rent free and coal provided! At one time there was a craze for low water in the moors to grow more food and a government official was sent round to see how to keep it low. He soon discovered that I was the man who controlled the water and I had to stand on my head sometimes to do it. Some farmers wanted it low but others didn't and if they were having it tough then watch out. I had to steer a chalk line to keep them happy. I don't know that flooding is as damaging as some might imagine.

Steam is a partnership between the driver and engine and this one was the simplest you could have. It would speak to you and all it needed was the oil can. It could lift 60 tons of water a minute and when the moors flooded I was out of bed at 4 a.m. and finishing at midnight, working 20 hours a day for eight to ten days. I could shift some water in that time!

Walter Musgrave. 'Water's in my blood, but I hope it's not on my brain!'

Oiling the steam pump, Westonzoyland Engine Trust.

The Parish of Burrow Bridge was only recently formed. The map reveals the names of a number of one-time farms along the river bank, the prettiest and grandest being Manor Farm on the south bank. Notice, too, the Ebenezer Chapel of 1836, beating hands down its Church of England rival next to the bridge for architectural grace.

There is another pumping station on the south bank of the river. This was built to keep water off Salt Moor, the name suggesting the saline quality of the water in times of flood. The Parrett and the Tone have a high tidal reach and the rivers drop only about a foot for every mile they traverse. When a high tide meets heavy rainfall from the hills then the water becomes land locked and has only one place to go: it spills over the river banks and onto the moors.

Follow the road past Moorland House. Note the new wall built to strengthen the river bank. The road doglegs here but there is no right of way along the river. You stay on this lane to Westonzoyland. Near the end of Hoopers Lane you will see a sign for Westonzoyland Pumping Station which, if it is open, is worth a visit. This was the first station to be built and was up and running by 1836, its original engine replaced in 1861.

A charity now runs the station and no better collection of engines and enthusiasts can be found. I was amused to hear on my visit that the diesel engine next door, which made the 1861 Easton & Amos steam engine redundant after a staggering ninety years, is itself about to be replaced by an electric one!

As you walk towards the village, note the high bank to your left. This is known as Lake Wall and dates from the thirteenth century. At one time drainage from the King's Sedgemoor area flooded through a gap between Chedzoy and Westonzoyland finding the Parrett at Andersea, and the wall was built to protect the Weston Level and Earlake Moor. Later inhabitants found the wall a strong and safe haven for their houses.

Three generations of withy growers: Les, Michael and Jack Musgrove.
'I expect Jack will join the business, he keeps asking for a withy knife like Daddy's!'

On the right hand side of the lane is a chimney and osier boiler. The Musgrove family run a small business here growing withies, and they use Lake Wall to take advantage of the drying winds.

Walk into the village, past the Sedgemoor Inn and round to the church of St Mary the Virgin.

Westonzoyland, like its sisters Middlezoy and Othery, is built on higher ground that at one time was an island surrounded by marsh. Their very names translate to the western, middle and other settlement on the Island of Sowy.

It is hard to pinpoint just when this 'island' was first settled but certainly the monks of Glastonbury were taking advantage of the rich alluvial soil as early as the eighth century. If you have been wondering how such a small village came to have such a huge church then the link with Glastonbury is the answer. By the thirteenth century Westonzoyland had reclaimed a great deal of land for both pasture and arable and with it came prosperity and a growth in population. There are records of a chapel here in 1268, its chancel looked after by the Abbot, but the present building is largely due to the enthusiasm of Richard Beere, the Abbot of Glastonbury from 1493 to 1524. Its bench ends, the richly carved angel roof bathed in light from its clerestory and its huge tower dominating this part of Somerset make the exploration of the church an absolute delight. There is a well written leaflet to guide you round but also have a look at the roof boss over the font in the south aisle. I lay on the floor and examined it through binoculars. The carving is of a dragon creature eating its tail but I cannot decide whether the blob resting on its middle is a pear, or something more sinister!

If the architectural splendour of the church doesn't move you, then this tale will. The Monmouth Rebellion of 1685, the pistol shot in the night that ruined the chance of a change in government, and the subsequent bloodbath on the outskirts of the village is a story well told, but some 500 of his men, many wounded and dying, were herded like cattle and locked inside

Angel roof, Westonzoyland church.

the church. How frightened they must have been, with the charge of treason and the threat of the gallows hanging over their heads.

A visit to the memorial on the site of the battlefield is a necessary diversion not only for the atmosphere of the place but also for its kind, yet careful, dedication. Leave the churchyard by the stile on the north wall, turn left into the lane and about 50 yards on your right join the footpath marked as a cycle route. Notice the paddocks that border this path. They are a remnant of plots so typical of the medieval period and if you study the map you will see how they stretch out in long narrow strips behind each house.

Turn right onto the lane and follow the road round to Bussex Farm. The memorial is well signposted and about half a mile down the drove. Other important battles that shaped the nation are remembered here, but I particularly like the two trees that were planted at the dedication ceremony in 1927. In a photograph of the event they appear as saplings surrounded by painted wrought iron guards. Today, although huge, they are still enclosed by their nursery protectors!

You can either retrace your steps to Bussex Farm and then on to Liney or carry on down to King's Sedgemoor Drain, turning right to the footbridge and follow the path to Liney from there. It will extend the walk by two miles but the Drain is impressive. On the winter's day that we walked it, we counted no fewer than fifty cormorants sitting on the electricity cables. Word must have got round that the Drain was full of fish!

King's Sedgemoor Drain is a landmark to the greatest change on the levels since the time of the monasteries. Completed in 1795, it illustrates the movement of parliamentary enclosure and agricultural improvement that swept the country in the latter part of the eighteenth century. King's Sedgemoor had been described as a disgrace insomuch that it was only fit for grazing three or four months of the year. In 1791 an act was passed to drain and divide the land. The River Cary was diverted in the east and the channel cut across the centre of the moor to an outfall at Dunball. It was not without its problems. There were plenty of objections from the commoners who stood to lose their rights, and it is thought that because of wrangling with landowners at the Parrett end the choice of Dunball for the clyse (a local name for a tidal lock) was a poor compromise. However, in latter years, the drain has been widened and deepened, the greatest improvement happening in the late thirties with a larger cut through the coastal clay belt.

From Liney take the road in a southerly direction to the east end of the village and cross over the main road to a drove directly opposite. Follow this round into Langmead. There is a choice of paths to Middlezoy but I recommend the one straight across the moor. The one to your left skirts the old airfield but also passes under the nose of a gypsy camp and, whilst it is a right of way, you may not get on with their dogs.

Two thirds of the way along the drove take the path on your left across two fields and join the track at the foot of Rowland's Hill. Immediately on your right is a small footbridge across a ditch and into the field. Take this, as the track can be very muddy and it cuts off the corner. At the top of the hill stay in the field and walk towards the village. The view from here is wonderful as you can see Middlezoy church one way and, being high, look back over the moor to Westonzoyland.

The church of the Holy Cross, perched on the highest ground overlooking the village, has a pleasing and soothing presence. Inside it appears quite plain at first, especially compared to the splendour of Westonzoyland, but look around and its delights are soon revealed. In the south aisle is a fine example of medieval stained glass depicting the martyr St Dorothy and, although crude, it has a special charm.

The pulpit of 1606 is not the best example I have seen but it is interesting to note that two bench ends in the nave, almost hidden as they butt up against the pillars of the south aisle, are carved by the same man, and are not contemporary with the others. Two other bench ends have interesting carvings, the figure of the man especially so as his dress is unusual.

The delicate oak screen to the chancel is attributed to the time of Abbot Richard Beere, though the claim that the small carving depicting two entwined ears of corn forms the letter 'R' is debatable.

My favourite furnishing in this church is the misericord (a special type of seat in a choir stall) and is found on the south side of the chancel. Contemporary with the medieval bench ends, its hinged seat has a fine carving of a dragon with a

Bench end, Middlezoy church.

Misericord, Middlezoy church.

serpent in its mouth and, below, a small human head. The misericord (meaning compassion) was designed so that you could perch your rear whilst appearing to stand. How very thoughtful! Nowadays a discreet electric heater is often added to increase the comfort.

Again there is a good church guide, which I urge you to buy as sales help to support the fabric fund, but once again look at the bosses on the ceiling. I missed it on my first visit but at the western end of the north aisle is a carving of two figures caught in a rather embarrassing sexual embrace.

As you leave the church notice the unusual graffiti carved into the polished lias of the porch seats. Like Cinderella, the culprits would not have escaped for long!

Walk down into the village. The mixture of old and new, with working farms still in the centre, gives it a pleasant air and a feeling that it has not yet been taken over by the commuter. At the end of Church Road turn left and take the path on your right up the flight of concrete steps. Follow this to the next lane and then take the footpath out into the fields to Othery. The path zigzags around the meadows and over foot bridges until you meet a well defined drove. Follow this until you see the path through the long field towards the church.

At the end of the field the footpath takes you over two stone stiles skirting the eastern brick wall of what was once the kitchen garden of Othery Rectory. Modern times have dictated economies within the church and the older large rectories, which were cold and expensive to run, have been sold off. In this case part of the garden provided space for a new rectory.

Cross the lane and by the telephone box join the path known as 'the Twist'. The church of St Michael has unfortunately suffered from repeated attacks by vandals and is kept locked. This is ironic when you think how in the past Cromwell's followers desecrated so many churches, pulling the statues from the niches of the towers. Those at St Michael's have survived. (It is possible to borrow the church key from the Rectory if the parson is at home.)

Built on the cruciform pattern, the church is well worth a visit. Notice the odd squint in the buttress of the tower, probably made to let more light into the chancel. (The window was glazed with stained glass in Victorian times.)

Cross over the A361 and go down Rye Lane by the London Inn. This joins Summerhedge Road and takes you down to Pathe. You are right on the southern tip of the 'island' now and there are good views to the wooded slopes of Turn Hill across the moors to the east. It is interesting to ponder that thousands of years ago the ridge was the cliff to the sea.

As the road bends round to the right, Aller Drove is to your left and the footpath to Stathe is immediately in front of you. Keep the ditch to your right and walk out onto the moor. Southlake Moor, although very low lying, was reclaimed by the monks of Glastonbury in the thirteenth century. At this time the Parrett had a number of fisheries in the form of weirs which seriously hampered the drainage of the moors in times of flood. The answer was to straighten and build up the sides of the river with strong embankments and also build flood prevention walls to encircle the rest of the moor. What is now called Burrow Wall runs from Pathe to the Mump, skirting the A361 and another wall runs from Pathe along our path to Stathe and the Parrett.

The importance of these walls and the land they came to protect is well documented in an incident involving a certain Matthew de Clevedon of Allermoor in 1311. He threw down part of Southlake Wall and consequently flooded some 1350 acres of land on the Sowy Moors. It was claimed that a thousand acres of corn, beans and peas were flooded, a fascinating insight into medieval agricultural activity.

Cross over the Parrett at Stathe and follow the lane back to Burrow Bridge. The embankment of the Parrett gives a fine view of the Mump and its church reflected on the surface of the river.

Before you finish your walk look over the bridge at the confluence of the Parrett and the Tone. There is a strange marker on the river bank and you may have noticed others at the start of the walk. A plastic milk carton supported on a stick is the secret sign of the elver fisherman, staking his claim to that particular patch and warning others to stay clear.

Adult eels were an important part of the medieval diet and the monasteries grew fat on the catch. Today it is their fry, the elver, that has become the prize and when the season starts there is a scramble for the river-bank. Smaller than a garden worm, they are caught by the netful and provide a welcome income for both the would-be and full time fisherman.

The River Parrett in winter flood. Stathe.

The life cycle of the eel is truly fascinating and is one of those great mysteries of nature. An adult eel will leave its muddy home of ditch and rhyne and swim hundreds of miles to the place of its birth. The Sargasso Sea lies in the mid-Atlantic, between the West Indies and the Azores, and it is here that the eels come to spawn from rivers in Europe and North America. The sea takes its name from the seaweed that floats on its surface and the waters are calm: ideal conditions for the millions of drifting eggs. Once hatched the elvers begin their journey across the ocean and by the end of winter they arrive in their thousands, a seething shoal of thin transparent bodies with ghostly black eyes, moving up river on the night tide.

Locally the elvers used to be hailed as a delicacy, fried in butter and served with scrambled egg, but the value of the catch is the driving force behind the fishing. They are sold by the kilo, at night, at a clandestine rendezvous with a refrigerated van and are then flown to Europe. Whether they are eaten over there or used to stock their rivers is of little interest to the fisherman, but the quantity they catch comes in for heavy criticism by the conservationist. The fisherman argues that he is going about a legal business, licensed by the National Rivers Authority.

I spent an evening with an elverman and, far from appearing greedy, he told me of his solution to the problem of over fishing. It made good sense to me and ought to be taken up.

> The NRA hand out all these licences so why don't they take a percentage of each night's catch, and stock the rhynes and ditches. I wouldn't mind, and that way the eels could finish their journey and everybody's happy.

Elver fishing on the River Parrett.

28

Winter flood on West Sedgemoor.

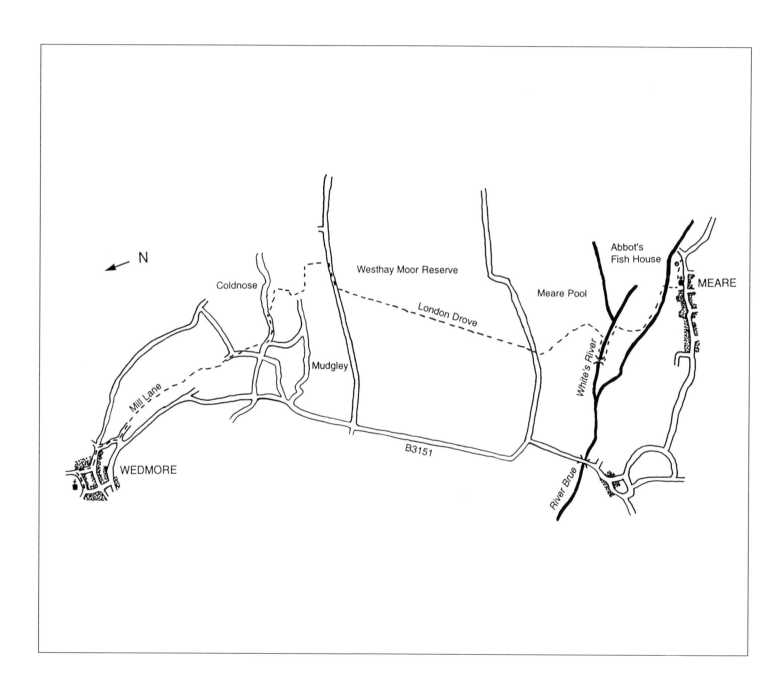

N

Coldnose

Westhay Moor Reserve

London Drove

Mudgley

Mill Lane

B3151

WEDMORE

Abbot's
Fish House

Meare Pool

MEARE

White's River

River Brue

WALK THREE

A Sanctuary for Birds:

MEARE TO WEDMORE VIA THE WESTHAY RESERVE

(Pathfinder map 1218 or Explorer 4) 6 miles.

Another island settlement on the marshland of the Levels, the name Meare simply translates to lake and refers to Meare Pool, a large expanse of water that once existed to the north of the village. The island belonged to Glastonbury Abbey and the importance of the pool as a source of fish is evidenced by the surviving Abbot's Fish House.

The building was erected in the reign of Edward III, probably at the same time as the neighbouring Manor House, during the abbacy of Adam de Sodbury (1322 to 1335). It was once two-storeyed with the upper living quarters reached by an external staircase. Downstairs the fisherman would have dried, salted and stored the fish. Unfortunately a fire in the nineteenth century destroyed the fine timber roof but a similar design can be found in the chancel of the church of St Mary. The Fish House stands on what was once the south-west shore of the lake which after the Dissolution was gradually drained for meadow. By the early eighteenth century it had completely disappeared.

Pass by the Abbot's Lodgings – a wonderful building with a weathered effigy of an abbot above the main entrance porch. This building, now Manor Farm, was used as a retreat by the Glastonbury abbots, though one imagines it must have been a chilly place in winter when the northerly winds blew over the lake. It was extended and re-furbished in the early sixteenth century by Richard Beere, an abbot whose taste for good

building is in evidence across the levels. Note the fine ecclesiastical doorway in the shippon.

This is a working farm with a fine dairy herd of Friesians so you will have to persevere with the path. It will be the one time you will wish you had your wellies! The path goes through the farmyard and down over a fine stone bridge across the River Brue. In the summer look out for huge chub lazing in the weed.

As you walk down river you can clearly see how Meare developed along a ridge, with long field strips bordered by deep ditches to facilitate the draining of the land. One field has a large stone circle, but don't be fooled for it is not as old as it looks.

Continue down river and, once you have passed a clump of willow trees in a small depression in the middle of the field, strike out for the north-west corner and pass through an iron gateway. Unfortunately, the footbridge across White's River is no longer with us, but don't despair. Continue west and you will come to a pillbox and a tree at a junction of White's River and a rhyne, and over a wooden gate you will see another bridge. Cross over and then walk back towards the pillbox and then head north-east along the rhyne until you pick up the path. There is a good hard track from the metal-framed barn, under the electricity pylons and out onto the road.

The Abbot's Fish House, Meare.

Churchyard and door, Meare.

Many farms on the levels are not ring-fenced, that is their land is scattered over a large area. Historically, this reflects the piecemeal pattern of farming when stock had to be moved around in times of flooding. If you are in milk it is far simpler to bring the mountain to Mohammed: sometimes a mobile milking bail is moved from one field to another with the cows. Stan Jones of Godney still milks in this way.

I started when I was eight or nine years old, to have to milk a cow, by hand of course, and I've been doing it for sixty years. You could only milk six by hand and then your wrists would give out. When the machine came in it made it easier work but this is a job you have to do, twice a day, regardless. I start at half-five, milking at six and give way a bit in the winter when it's a cold morning. Your bail goes with the cows and your cows goes with the fields, so we're off the road 'til we want to move.

They're tightening the knot now on dairying and everything's so different from what it used to be but I'd rather have the levels than the hills. It's open country, the air's good here, what do you want better?

My son has started digging peat, he's not keen on milking. We started because the rest is digging the land around us, we got to. It's drying the land out. I think it's a bad thing because the generation of children that's born today, they'll come along and they'll have no business in years to come. A lot of the land's going to be gone – dug out to peat. There's nothing left but water. And rubbish.

Stan Jones and his milking bail, Godney.

Stan Jones.

*Stan Jones. 'The air's good here,
what do you want better?'*

As you walk across the fields you gain an impression of what Meare Pool must have looked like – a huge expanse of water five miles in circumference. Once it was drained the loss of birdlife, especially wildfowl, had a considerable effect on the local economy. In order to compensate for this a system of decoy pools was built. The ducks would land on the ponds and being naturally curious would swim up into channels that were netted overhead. The fowler would spring out from behind and frighten the birds into flight along the channel and into the narrowing net. Although numbers caught were impressive the decoy survives only as a name on the map. Perhaps the absence of sportsmanship led to its decline and today duck shooting, usually by boat during the winter floods, is the only surviving tradition.

Cross over the road and onto London Drove. You are now on Westhay Moor which has been extensively worked for its deep deposits of peat. Formerly a raised peat bog, it was designated as the Somerset Trust Westhay Reserve in 1995. The area is now a mixture of reed fen, sallow carr, meadow, heath and bog, criss-crossed with channels and a number of lakes. The place is alive with birds and a haven for all manner of wildlife and plants. Throughout the year you can be guaranteed to see coots, moorhens, herons and swans with the occasional blue flash of the kingfisher lifting the scene. In winter the numbers and species of wildfowl increase. Towards nightfall there is also a spectacular though deafening scene, reminding one of Hitchcock's *The Birds*, as up to a quarter-of-a-million starlings come in to roost. They pay for this disturbance when they are swooped upon the next morning by the watchful sparrowhawk.

There are a number of hides and screens on the site and viewing is best done during still weather as in strong winds many birds shelter in the reed. I've seen crested grebe here and even the little egret. If you sit and wait patience is usually rewarded.

There are a number of bodies who have funded the site. Until 1994 the Somerset Wildlife Trust owned 110 acres. Part of their purchase was funded by English Nature, the Worldwide Fund for Nature, the European Community and the British Wildlife Appeal. In 1994 Levingtons Horticulture gifted a further 147 acres of old peat workings which were converted to wetland with a grant from the European Community.

The site does not stand still and requires constant management. In the centre of the reserve 12 acres of woodland which have invaded over the last forty years are being clear felled. It is hoped that the original raised bog lost by the lowering of the water table during the peat digging will be restored.

Westhay Moor is important for the raised bog plant communities. Sphagnum moss, cotton grass, sedges, sundew and the royal fern are all found here. Although you are unlikely to see them, there are also a number of rare invertebrates with resounding names such as the Great Raft Spider and Bog Bush Cricket.

Peat digging still continues around the reserve and if left alone the water table would continue to fall. Trees are highly efficient water pumps drawing the accumulated rainfall out of the peat and allowing it to evaporate via the leaf surface. By sealing the edges of the reserve to prevent run-off and removing some of the trees the situation can be reversed.

As you leave the reserve at the end of London Drove turn right and walk past Stan Sweet's Landscaping with the delightful mixture of vegetable plot, nursery and scrapyard. On your left you will come to a galvanised iron gate supported by two sleepers, the left hand one painted with a small red dot. Walk across the field to the double gates across the rhyne (one is painted white) then straight up to the long hedge and join the path to Mudgley House Farm.

The farmhouse and cottages are dated 1847 and 1877 and are monogrammed with the same initials, presumably indicating an expanding farming family.

Bird watching on London Drove.

Restoration of the raised bog, Westhay Reserve.

Between the houses is a small lane up to Bagley. Half way up the hill is a stile and although this is not our path climb over and enjoy the view. You can now see the extent of the reserve as the sky reflects off the lakes with Meare and the Polden Hills beyond.

At the top of the hill take the track on your left and walk diagonally across the field towards Coldnose with the two-tiered bungalow to your right. Coldnose is an apt description. You are now on a thin windswept ridge and as you walk across the field the view opens up to a breathtaking scene revealing the Quantocks right round to Glastonbury and on to the long stretch of the Mendips with Crooked Peak in the distance and the distinctive hill of Nyland bulging out of the levels below.

Pass over the stile by an old oak tree and turn left up the lane. The '60s Bagley Baptist Chapel is a period piece but I can't share in a love some people have for the architecture. Opposite the turning for Mudgley there is a wooden break in the hedge; climb over and cut across the field to Townsend Lane. As you approach the end of the field you can now pick out the west front of Wells Cathedral. Don't follow Townsend Lane down the hill but go straight ahead. A little further on the track splits into two and you have a choice. Mill Lane is the quieter and will keep you off the busy B3151. I imagine this track was once a drove road to the moors and for a brief moment one rain-soaked afternoon I felt what it must have been like to drive the animals along. The water lashed down in vertical sheets and the mud cloyed to my boots.

At the end of the track turn right into Mutton Lane and walk down into Wedmore. I recommend visiting the church first then walking back down to the Borough for afternoon tea.

Wedmore was once a royal estate of the Saxon kings and it was here that the Danish King Guthrum signed the peace treaty with Alfred. The parish church of St Mary stands above the older part of the village and is similar in design to that of North Curry. There is much to see inside and if the end of your walk is bright and sunny the interior will glow with colourful light. The huge west window of stained glass commemorates the Golden Jubilee of Queen Victoria with an attempt at establishing her importance with more notable events of the past. The three monarchs who also attained jubilees are depicted at the top by the heads of Henry III, Edward III and George III. Below are four full length panels showing Alfred burning the cakes and the rites following Guthrum's baptism at Aller, Harold's oath and his death at Hastings, Elizabeth I with Sir Walter Raleigh and below them the Spanish Armada, and Victoria's coronation in 1837 and her family fifty years later.

There is also an expensive brass plaque on the wall of the north aisle which I find rather pretentious. It reads; 'Erected by Robert Edmund Dickenson MP in the first year of King Edward VII being the thousandth year from the death of King Alfred the Great. 901-1901'. How lucky the dates coincided!

I appear to be scathing, but there are parts of this church that I love. The corbels that hold the roof are all a mixture of carved stone kings, queens and beasts. For the most part nobody is looking terribly jolly, but I think the mason was enjoying his work. The south chapel corbels have a pelican and two entwined dolphins and if you look closely you can see traces of red and white paint on the ceiling woodwork. Perhaps the entire roof was at one time painted.

Behind the Jacobean pulpit is a sixteenth century fresco of St Christopher with Jesus on his back and a mermaid and ships at his feet. It is delightful in its simplicity and originally would have been painted with pigmented limewash giving it a soft and gentle glow. Unfortunately it appears to have been reworked and sealed with an ugly varnish.

St Mary's church, Wedmore.

The jolly abbot, Wedmore church.

In the north chapel are two brass plaques to the Hodge family one of which reads well: 'Wounded, not Vanquished. Sacred to the memory of Captain Thomas Hodges in the county of Somerset Esq who at the siege of Antwerp about 1583 with unconquered courage won two ensigns from the enemy, where receiving his last wound he gave three legacies. His soul to his Lord, his body to be lodged in Flemish earth and his heart to be sent to his dear wife in England. Here lies his wounded heart for whom one kingdom was too small a room, two kingdoms therefore have thought good to part so stout a body and so brave a heart.'

Leave the Church and walk down to the Borough. At the bottom of the hill, and now occupied by a chemist's, is a fine Italianate building erected in the nineteenth century by John Tonkin (his name can still be seen on the brass window sills). He built it for his lady friend whom he brought from Italy and installed here. She was a great follower of fashion and before long had established Tonkin's as a major fashion house. There used to be a tower behind the main façade where the ladies would go and sip tea after being fitted for their hats and dresses.

A lady born in the village told me that when she was small the shop became a store where everything was available from the cradle to the grave, literally. You could buy furniture, it had a little bank and the top storey was full of buckets and tombstones!

The tea rooms of the Borough Venture continue the tradition of Tonkins. I suggest you leave your boots at the door for here again is a fashion house with a very smart carpet. It sells a range of ladies' garments from some of Europe's leading design houses with sizes ranging from a tiny 8 to a generous 24. It is all a little odd after the walk, though far from intimidating. The tea and cakes are excellent. If you need to be brought back to earth with an old sense of place then the fourteenth-century market cross stands just across the road!

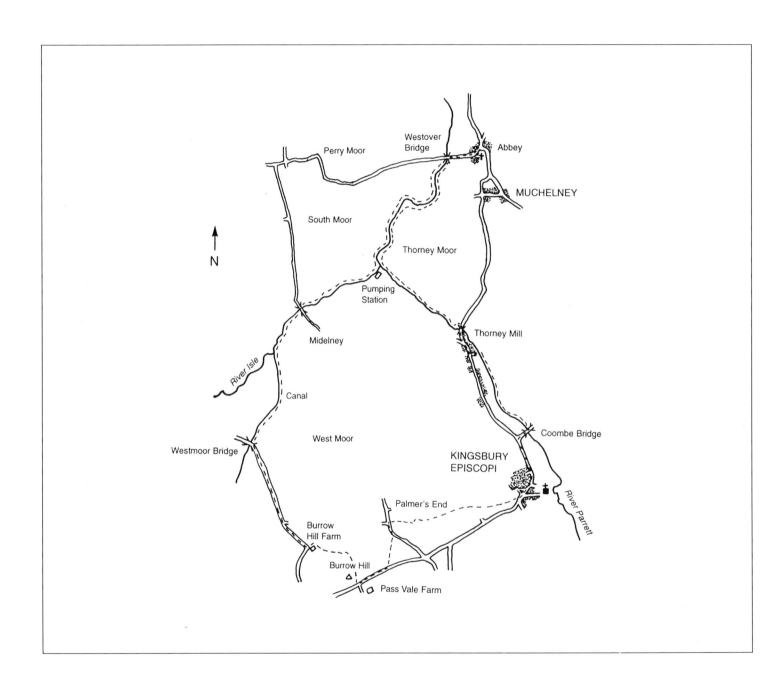

Perry Moor

Westover
Bridge

Abbey

MUCHELNEY

South Moor

Thorney Moor

N

Pumping
Station

River Isle

Midelney

Thorney Mill

Canal

West Moor

Coombe Bridge

Westmoor Bridge

KINGSBURY
EPISCOPI

River Parrett

Palmer's End

Burrow
Hill Farm

Burrow Hill

Pass Vale Farm

WALK FOUR

Cider and Monastery:

KINGSBURY EPISCOPI, BURROW HILL, MIDELNEY, MUCHELNEY, THORNEY MILL, KINGSBURY EPISCOPI

(Pathfinder map 1259) 9 miles.

Mentioned in the Domesday Book, Kingsbury Episcopi, as the name indicates, was once in the possession of the Bishop of Bath and Wells and was probably made over to him as an endowment from one of the Saxon kings in the tenth century. It was a spiritual age and the Christian institutions often benefited from a generous monarchy.

The village is built on the compacted soils of the Parrett, the church of St Martin claiming the land closest to the river bank. The exterior of the church is truly handsome and its four-stage tower and honey-coloured hamstone will take your breath away. Sadly the interior has the opposite effect and, apart from a nicely carved rood screen across the chancel and a fan vaulted ceiling in the tower, I feel it has little to commend it.

In the mid-nineteenth century the church had fallen into serious decay and was the subject of extensive renovation. It was all carried out with the best of intentions but the end result is unattractive. Looking around St Martin's I realised why. In the north chapel a small amount of the original ceiling survives. Compare this with the restored roof in the chancel and nave. The Victorians had powered machinery at their disposal giving the new woodwork a sharp clean edge with perfect symmetry. The hand carved charm of the old roof has been lost.

After visiting the church, walk past the old house with the precarious leaning chimney and take the footpath to the right of the Wyndham Arms. Note the old cycling club sign above the door.

The footpath soon leaves the village behind and crosses a number of fields before stepping over Hitchings Drove and joining a small hedge-lined track. Follow this in a straight line and then cross the fields, through the remnants of an old orchard and on to Palmer's End. The footpath comes out onto the Middle Drove in front of the tall Victorian cottage.

Turn left and, ignoring the lane to Lower Burrow, follow the road towards Stembridge. At Palmer's End bungalow, marked by a red milk churn in the garden, there is a tiny footbridge over the ditch by the wall on your right. This is the official footpath up into the field and on to Burrow Way *if* you can squeeze through! Alternatively walk to the left of the bungalow and join the field via the farmyard.

Walk straight up the middle of the field (the hedge on the map has been grubbed out) and head towards the single-chimneyed cottage on Burrow Way. Walk up the lane to Pass Vale Farm.

This is the home of Julian Temperley, a man passionate about good cider and, lately, the English answer to Calvados. You may wish to purchase some cider to take on your walk or visit by car later. The farm is open for sales throughout the year.

St Martin's church, Kingsbury Episcopi.

May Queen, Kingsbury Episcopi.

May Day, Kingsbury Episcopi.

It is difficult to pinpoint just when cider production started in Somerset. The Celts certainly grew apples as did the Romans and although written evidence is scanty, it seems likely that the art is very old. In the seventeenth century the drink had caught on with orchard planting throughout the county. Many farms had their own press and it became common practice to pay the wages partly in drink. It has to be remembered that farm work, even up to the Second World War, was extremely labour intensive with long hours of monotonous work in the fields. Any farmhand will tell you that even today a gallon of cider in the hayfield is a welcome friend. The drink is thirst quenching and, rather than becoming blind drunk, the body slips into a happy rhythm of work.

As a drink real cider had suffered a bad press but is now making a comeback. During this century commercial cider making took over from the farms, due mainly to the decline in farm labour. Factory produced carbonated cider led people to believe that it had always been crystal clear, clean tasting and fizzy. Coupled with this, the farmhouse scrumpy sold in the public house sat around in its plastic barrels for far too long and consequently put a lot of people off.

Cider is made by the careful blending of different apple varieties. Delightful names such as Porters Perfection and Slack-ma-Girdle tell of their individual reputations and they vary widely in their acid and tannin content. Court Royal for instance is described as a sweet, and is low in acidity and tannin, whereas the Kingston Black is a bittersharp and the acidity and tannin are high. The varieties also have a bearing on harvest time and the season for production can run from October to as late as Christmas.

Once harvested the apples are washed and then crushed to produce a pulp known as the pomace. This is then spread onto cloths and built up in layers to produce the 'cheese' which in turn is slowly squashed in a hydraulic press. The extracted juice is then pumped into wooden barrels and the naturally

*Picking cider apples, North Curry. In larger orchards
the apples are usually picked up by machine.*

Building the 'cheese' for cider, Burrow Hill.

Pressing cider apples, North Curry. At one time most farms would have had a press similar to this.

Burrow Hill summit.

present yeasts of the apple begin the fermentation. To aid clarification and once fermentation has ceased, the liquid is racked from the exhausted yeast. The result is a strong, still and dry cider (which can only be sweetened by the addition of sugar).

The science has changed very little over the years but the mechanics have. At one time horses would have been used in harness, crushing the apples via a stone mill. Later the smaller farms used hand cranked machines, but today the crusher is belt driven from either a tractor, stationary engine or electric motor. Long straw was used to build the cheese and the press was screwed down by hand.

If you taste good cider, and Temperley's certainly is one of Somerset's best, its bad reputation should be laid to rest. The blending of apples and careful production and storage are all part of an art. Like wine it doesn't keep once exposed to the air and if you purchase a gallon in a plastic container it will deteriorate in a matter of days. I often decant it into glass bottles which lengthens its shelf life considerably. Alternatively you can buy pasteurised cider which is also excellent and will keep for longer.

Cider brandy had not been licensed in England for over three hundred years when in 1984 the late Bertram Bulmer was allowed to distil cider in Hereford. This was not on a commercial scale and was part of a museum attraction so in 1987 the Temperleys pushed for a licence. Marketed under the name Somerset Royal it has gained a considerable reputation with its own distinct character. The liquid is distilled during the winter and then aged in oak barrels for a number of years to develop its colour and depth. The Temperleys fought long and hard for the licence but the rules state that you are not allowed to distil on the same premises where you make the cider. In a grand show of trust Her Majesty's Customs and Excise hold the keys to the distillery some two miles down the road!

Leaving the farm turn left until you reach a wooden gate to Burrow Hill. The view from the top is stunning and the shapely sycamore growing on the summit provides a good landmark on the rest of the walk.

When you come off the hill struggle over the fence alongside the row of poplars (not marked on the map) and follow the hedge to the bottom of the field. In the corner is a stile out onto the abandoned track of Way Ridge. Immediately on your left there is a small gate in the hedge. Go through and follow the hedge to the right until you come to a fence stile. Go down the field to Burrow Hill Farm. The footpath shown on the OS map has long since gone but the farmer will allow you to pass through the yard immediately behind the house. Watch out for dogs and remember it is private.

Once on New Road walk in a northerly direction across West Moor to Westmoor Bridge and turn right onto the canal path. Again the OS map is wrong here but the footpath is clearly waymarked to Midelney (pronounced Mid'ney).

In 1833 West Moor was one of the last moors to be reclaimed and made good use of the experience gained in other parts of the Levels. The usual network of rhynes led into a central drain some 3 miles long which now ends at a pumping station at the confluence of the rivers Isle and Parrett. Withies proved to be one of the most successful crops in the newly-reclaimed moor and were planted on a grand scale. If you study the present map, however, many of the fields that are marked as Osiers (withy beds) have now disappeared. Today there are only a few beds left, one of which, near Pitt Bridge, has been let go to provide cover for wildlife. Grant-aided by English Nature, they also gave grants to grub them out (!), hoping to encourage the return of flowers and grasses that once colonised the meadows.

Roy White cleaning his ditches on West Moor. 'This meadow used to be a withy bed but I got a grant to grub it out. Now all the old flowers that have lain dormant for years are coming back.'

Westport Canal once linked the marine traffic from the Bristol Channel via the Rivers Parrett and Isle to Hambridge and Westport. Built in 1840 its history was brief, and it suffered severe problems with flooding on the moors and stiff competition from the railways. In a sad state of decay, Vagg's Bridge emphasises the canal's demise.

Although the traffic has gone, the canal serves a new purpose. The banks are well colonised with trees and plants and are a haven for wildlife. In winter the waters are muddy but in the dry summer of 1995 I enjoyed the sight of a young pike basking in the warm rays of sunlight illuminating the canal bed.

Further along the canal joins the River Isle and the copses of Midelney reveal higher ground. This 'island' has an interesting history. In the centre lies Midelney Manor, a simple Elizabethan house with a surviving falcon mews. The house was originally built as two, occupied by brothers who couldn't agree. The manor was originally held by Muchelney Abbey and it is claimed that the Trevilian family, whose descendants occupy the present house, were tenants of the monks. With the closure of the abbey in 1538 the family bought the freehold. The house is open to the public every Thursday afternoon in summer from 2.30 p.m. until 4.30 p.m. and the present Trevilian gives a splendid and humorous tour. I will leave him to tell you of Richard and Thomas and their petty squabble!

From Midelney Bridge continue along the west bank of the Isle towards Muchelney. After the charm of Midelney Manor the Westmoor Pumping Station sits as a blot on the landscape, the 1960s functional design ending there. It represents, however, the latest phase in the battle to control the flooding and houses an electrically driven pump which works automatically as the need arises. It is likely that all the pumping stations on the Levels will one day adopt a similar system.

James Palmer with his Red-Tailed Buzzard, Midelney.

John Trevilian of Midelney Manor.

Muchelney Abbey in its 'island' setting.

The next stretch is very pleasant. The Isle has now joined the Parrett and the country opens up to wide views over Thorney Moor. The path goes over the bed of the redundant Taunton to Yeovil railway and on to Westover Bridge, crossing the Parrett and into Muchelney. The village has grown some distance from the abbey ruins, leaving the site with its atmosphere intact.

The island of Muchelney would have been everything a hermit could wish for, surrounded by marshland and isolated. There was a monastic house here in earlier Saxon times but the present foundation dates from a revival in the tenth century. The abbey of Muchelney was of the Benedictine Order and the excavated footings show the extent of the site. The surviving abbot's lodgings incorporate the south cloister walk and adjoin what was once the refectory. To the south-east is a thatched reredorter which should lay claim to be the prettiest toilet in Somerset!

The rule of St Benedict with the three obligations of poverty, chastity and obedience did not survive long and monastic houses like this soon became richly endowed. The Domesday Book records a vineyard, two fisheries producing an annual return of 6000 eels, 25 acres of meadow and 100 acres of pasture, with 21 cattle, six pigs and 30 goats. These were not great assets but by the fourteenth century a picture emerges of a religious house rather lax in its ways. The abbot was reprimanded for the luxuries that he and his monks enjoyed. They slept in private rooms instead of the dormitory, ate from expensive plate and wandered in and out as they pleased. As a churchwarden pointed out to me 'They may have worshipped God but they certainly had a jolly good time!'

Just how jolly is related in the following recent poem by James Crowden.

ANOTHER EARLY MORNING: CIRCA 1520 AD
Word has got around, goings on at the Abbey.

'... and not just new fireplaces either,
all that food and just for twenty?

I say, there must be more there
and not all the same shape and size.
And what was that about separate bedrooms?
All that rebuilding?
A place for seclusion alright
but whose paying for it, I ask?

Whose paying for it? All that land,
why they've got Midelney, and Thorney as well,
and what with the mill, they've got it all sewn up.
Shouldn't be allowed, that's what I say
and as for people creeping back to their villages
early in the morning ... say no More,
women ought to know better,
but when its frozen
and there's a little snow on the ground
you can follow their footprints,
from back door to back door.

The Abbot's grazing alright
but not just sheep,
if you follow my meaning...'

Religious houses loved to keep up with fashion. A rebuilding programme in the early sixteenth century brought the abbey to its knees and a lack of finance forced its closure in 1538, a few months before Henry would have dissolved it by law. Over the following centuries the stonework was sold off, though the lodgings and some buildings survived as a farm. Upstairs in the lodging is a beautiful fireplace, its overmantel carved with an entwining vine and quatrefoil frieze, with two ascending pillars topped by lions. Its rich and sumptuous design is a monument to the downfall of the abbey.

Painted ceiling, Muchelney church.

Salvaged carving, Muchelney Abbey.

Before leaving Muchelney the church of SS Peter and Paul is worth a visit if only to view the unusual wagon roof. Cheerfully painted, it depicts the friendly face of the sun surrounded by adoring angels in Tudor costume with messages of 'Come up hether' and 'Fly to mercye.' The church was founded to serve the needs of the villagers and a priest installed in the house opposite. Although not under the jurisdiction of the abbey the priest was well looked after with most of his meals supplied by the abbey kitchen. The fine fourteenth-century Priest's House is now in the hands of the National Trust.

Retrace your steps to Westover Bridge and now take the east bank of the Parrett in a southerly direction to Thorney Bridge. Once reached the OS map claims a path through the garden of the bungalow but skirt the perimeter fence round to your left and out onto Thorney Road via the wooden field gate. A short walk south will bring you to Thorney Mill and back onto the east bank of the Parrett.

Thorney Mill has a charming air, its pale blue painted windows sitting well with its lias stonework. Built in 1824, most of its

*Evie Body of Thorney working on her sculpture
for the new Sainsbury's in Street.*

machinery is still intact and although in need of repair the 14-foot water wheel can still turn. Now a private residence, inside there are four huge grindstones where flour and animal feed were once milled. The weir has a lock beside it to raise the barges that navigated the river.

Follow the footpath along the river to Coombe Bridge. Turn left down Thorney Road and back into Kingsbury Episcopi, passing by the village green with its unusual hamstone lock up.

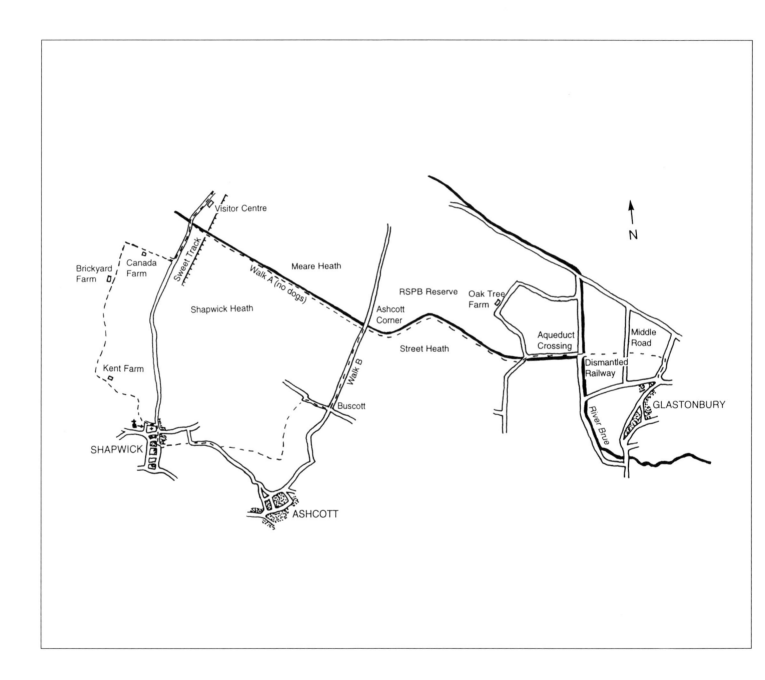

WALK FIVE

The Peatlands:

GLASTONBURY TO SHAPWICK

(Pathfinder map 1238 & 1218 or Explorer 4) 6 or 8 miles depending on the route.

I have offered two routes to Shapwick. One for dogs and their owners and a longer one strictly for *Homo sapiens*. I am afraid that if you bring your dog you will have to forgo Shapwick Heath and also the reconstructed Iron Age village at the visitor centre. This is because of otters which are disturbed by a dog's scent, and English Nature think it best to keep dogs from the heath.

At the Beckery roundabout in Glastonbury follow the sign for the industrial estate, down to a mini-roundabout; leave the three o'clock exit and park on the waste ground opposite Abbey Garage.

This is an odd view of Glastonbury Tor from the heart of an industrial estate, but for the purpose of this walk the contrast is a good one. The Tor symbolises what was once one of the most powerful and richest abbeys in England and today Glastonbury is a magnet for all manner of pilgrims. Some are drawn to the town as the cradle of English Christianity, while others come for the legend of King Arthur and the New Age culture.

But I want to leave all that behind. The land to the west of here is known locally as the peatlands, an odd mixture of industry and countryside. Conservation bodies now have a close eye on its future and the walk reveals past activity while taking you through the embryo stages of a restored landscape.

Opposite the mini-roundabout are the decaying gates and foot-bridge that once marked the crossing of Glastonbury's station. A short walk down this lane over the ditch leads you into the engineers' yard, and the associated buildings painted a dark green still survive as industrial units.

A retired porter, Jack Webb, still lives on the site in a wooden bungalow that was once the station master's office.

> This was a very busy place because every day we had a 60-truck peat train special come through here and five or six factories depended on us for their raw materials. Bason Bridge was a big depot for milk and it all came through Glastonbury. We had cattle come from Ireland, often late at night, so we used to unload them, put them into pens and water them, and then turn them out in the field behind. That's now a scrapyard! They were good old days but I was a few years younger then.

Retrace your steps to the mini-roundabout, noting on your left the dried up and overgrown cut that runs immediately behind one of the station buildings. This was the start of the Glastonbury Canal that at one time ran to Highbridge; we

Jack Webb, Retired Porter of Glastonbury Station.
'Mr Beeching wanted it closed.'

follow its course for part of our walk. Turn left back into Dye House Lane and follow the road round over an iron bridge and pick up the footpath on your left by the sign: 'Aqueduct Crossing 1 mile'. You now have a gentler view of Glastonbury with the church towers of St John the Baptist and St Benedict's dominating the roofline of the town.

Follow the footpath through the field, cross over Middle Road and continue through Lower New Close to the River Brue. On your left the dismantled railway bed of the Somerset and Dorset Railway now runs parallel to the old canal.

In the age of the motor car and heavy goods vehicle we forget that the major modes of transport have changed and may yet again. The canal was built in 1833 in order to import goods into Glastonbury via the Bristol Channel. Some 12 miles long and about 6 feet deep, its shallow-keeled barges carried items such as coal and slate from Wales. All over the country the railways were competing for the bargeman's trade and in 1847 a company bought the canal and by 1852 was using the route for its railway. Superseded by the faster form of transport the canal fell into decline and, apart from the occasional boat, served better as a drain for the surrounding land.

In turn Dr Beeching's axe in 1966 closed the Somerset and Dorset Railway and, without a thought for the future, the line was immediately ripped up and sold for scrap. Thirty years later we pollute ourselves, continue to run down the railways and invest all our money in the road network, blind to the fact that one day the country won't cope. Some years ago a friend commented on the loss of all these small rail routes and suggested that the central reservations of our larger roads could be used for a passenger rail. In Idaho the Americans are building Cybertran, a 150 m.p.h. train that will do just that, relieving traffic congestion into the city. We are a long way from such a solution but perhaps a form of rail network will once again cover the country.

Aqueduct Crossing.

The River Brue with Glastonbury Canal beyond.

When you reach the banks of the Brue turn left and cross over the redundant iron railway bridge. The name 'Ackyduct Crossing' was used fondly by the engine drivers but has nothing to do with the viaduct of the railway bridge. Turn right and walk along the river bank and you will notice a stone wall blocking the course of the canal. In order for it to continue it was necessary to build an aqueduct – hence the name. Judging by the water levels there must have been a system of locks, but the evidence is lost.

Take the lane signposted to Sharpham. You are now entering the peatlands and you will notice that the road is very uneven because of the nature of the subsoil. Past the first peatworks and at the next, Marshes Peat Products, notice a clay pigeon shooter's trap perched on top of the mound. The owner's daughter, Jo Marsh, won a gold medal in 1994 as the Ladies' World Sporting Champion, and at the age of seventeen was the youngest to take the title.

At end of lane you will see a phone box directly in front of you. Officially the route stays on the northern bank of the old canal but it is so unkempt that I recommend walking around to your left and following the bed of the old railway. Don't be put off by Wessex Water's signs of no right of way. They repeat the message further along while English Nature invite you to walk!

Follow this track to Ashcott Corner. All about you are the peat beds, some now redundant and hidden by plantlife, others heavily worked with lumps or mounds of peat stacked at the sides of deep black pits.

Peat has been cut for fuel from at least the Middle Ages and the abbey at Glastonbury would have made good use of this resource. It used to be cut by hand which made it very labour intensive.

Jo Marsh, 1994 Ladies' World Sporting Champion.

Jo Marsh and her father practising clay shooting at the peatworks.

Roger Rogers learned the art as did his father and grandfather before him:

> The peat was dug by hand with a turf scythe into lumps, or mumps as we called them, and then with a chopper they were split into three and the pieces were then known as turf. The pit is called a head and was measured by the amount of mumps that came out of it, and it was reckoned that two men could dig two thousand mumps in a day. As the turves became dry enough to handle they were put into what we called windrows and then built into ruckles, a sort of beehive shape. Most of the men did the digging and it was then down to the women and children to do the stacking jobs. It's only in the last thirty years, since the '60s, that the machines came in and as far as I know there's nobody cutting by hand any more.

The need for mechanisation of peat digging came about through the expansion of the horticultural industry and the growth in garden centres, and has speeded up extraction. Three different methods are used:

'Trench Cut' is similar to the hand method insomuch that the machine digs down to a depth of 3 feet and cuts the peat into blocks, ejecting them automatically into stacks to dry;

'Rotavation' turns the soil to a depth of about 6 inches and leaves the peat to dry. By this method three or four layers are extracted each year;

'Open Cast' uses the Hymac and bucket, and it is this method that allows the extraction of the full depth of peat down to the clay subsoil and well below the water table, requiring the use of pumps to keep the water at bay.

The speed at which the peat can now be extracted has caused great concern. If everyone extracted at the same rate it is estimated that there are only about twenty years of reserves left. It is argued that extraction not only loses agricultural land (as one farmer put it 'You are left with a big hole') but also has a serious effect on the wetland habitat.

Roger Rogers. 'Nobody digs peat by hand any more.'

Sally Mills of the RSPB planting reed rhizomes on their new reserve.

*Max King of Oak Tree Farm with his peat rotavator.
'I'd rather they kept tourism out and left us in peace.'*

Peat railtrack now used as a footbridge, Shapwick Heath.

Recognising the damage done by peat extraction, the RSPB have bought worked out peat diggings to the west of Oak Tree Farm and are now busy creating a marsh, planting reed rhizomes along the banks and keeping the water table high. They hope to attract breeding birds to their haven, including the bittern which has been absent from Somerset for many years.

There is a grand scheme eventually to turn the peatlands over to 'green tourism' and Somerset County Council has named this the Avalon Marshes Project. This isn't popular with everyone. Some farmers scratch their heads at all this activity and wish to be left in peace believing that nature will always fill the gaps without such interference. To be fair there is some truth in this and the old workings colonised by reed and fen shrub provide habitat for many different species of wildlife. It is the conservation bodies who wish to control the location and the type of habitat.

About $^3/_4$ mile on from Sharpham Crossing there is a small bridge across the bed of the canal. If you look closely on the concrete footings you will see that a railway once crossed here, used to move the blocks of peat around the diggings for loading onto the Somerset and Dorset. A little further on is a complete section of track now used as a footbridge.

On an August morning in 1949, a petrol driven locomotive belonging to the Eclipse Peat Company stalled on a crossing near Ashcott Corner. Unable to restart the engine or move his trucks, the driver ran down the line to try and warn the approaching 8 a.m. train from Glastonbury. Unfortunately it was foggy and he wasn't seen. The train ploughed into the peat locomotive, and its steam engine was derailed into the old canal. It proved impossible to retrieve her and she had to be cut up on the spot and scrapped.

Cross the railway bridge over the South Drain and you are now at Ashcott Corner.

(If you are with the dog follow the alternative route to Shapwick given below.)

Shapwick Heath is now a nature reserve and as such is a piece of heaven. Gone are the machines, and wildlife and plants can exist peacefully, disturbed only by the walker passing through. Further back on the walk you may have noticed some modern wooden planking laid across the peat to allow the Hymac access to the peatbeds. A version of this has been used before. Near the Shapwick Road the bed of the railway crosses over the Sweet Track, a Neolithic walkway discovered in 1970. Some six thousand years old, it connected the foothills of the Poldens with Westhay and in order to cross the swamp its builders laid long trunks of oak, ash and hazel across its surface, holding them together with large wooden pegs driven at an angle on either side. The Peat Moors Visitor Centre on the Shapwick Road has a reconstruction, as well as some convincing Iron Age huts of the lake village type. It is well worth a visit.

When you come out onto Station Road turn right for the visitor centre or left and continue the walk. In due course take the drove to your right past Canada Farm and join the Kent Drove which will take you all the way to Shapwick. The atmosphere is eerie on this stretch and I think it is because of the redundant farms. You can see the transition from farming to peatbed and nature reserve, and the latter now has a strong hold on the landscape. Here you will find fenwood and heath, alder-lined ditches and, just before you get to Brickyard Farm, a worked out peat digging flooded and full of reed mace – an amazing sight in winter as the bullrush heads sway in the wind and the duck jostle for the limited space on the water.

The drove carries on into open farmland and rises onto a hill with a copse that has the remains of an icehouse that once served Shapwick House.

From here the views are splendid as the end of the walk winds its way past Kent Farm and up into the village.

Shapwick has been the subject of an extensive survey to discover how it developed and although there is modern infill it is a pleasant village to explore. Its Saxon name refers to sheep and indicates the farming activity of that time on the Polden Hills.

In the tenth century it was part of the Glastonbury Abbey estate and at some point was subject to a reorganisation with the settlement laid out as a rectangular grid surrounded by open arable fields.

In the church of St Mary (a fourteenth-century building that replaced a Saxon church to the east) there is an eighteenth-century map showing the village layout. The open space in front of Shapwick House is now parkland but it is interesting to note the existence of houses and a road on the old map. The fashion for an uninterrupted view from the 'big house' certainly had its way here!

Alternative route for the dog owner

Set off down through Ashcott Heath, the most uneven road in Somerset and give thanks that walking doesn't make you seasick! The lovely little bungalow called Greenacre on your right is aptly named with its charming garden and wonky porch. The character of this stretch of the road doesn't feel like England at all and has an atmosphere more akin to the outback of Australia.

The soft peat soil is an obvious favourite with the mole and there is no chance for an immaculate lawn! As you begin to rise towards the Poldens the scene suddenly changes with an orchard on your left and cultivated pasture on your right. At the hamlet of Buscott turn sharp right into Buscott Lane and

Building a replica of the Sweet Track,
Peat Moors Visitor Centre, Shapwick Road.

walk along until the road doglegs. Then take the public footpath on your left into a field edge lined with oak trees. Follow the footpath into a little square field in between Buscott and Fifteen Acre Copse. You will need good map-reading skills here and a sharp eye to the way ahead. The footpath marked on the O.S. map cuts through the middle of a well established hedge and then alongside another that has been grubbed out!

Pretending that the grubbed out hedge is still there and keeping Millslade Hall well up to your left, cross the field and take the footbridge and stile in the right hand corner.

Climb the hill to the cottage with the line of fir trees protecting its orchard and turn right, following the track in a westerly direction to the Ashcott–Shapwick road. There are fine views from here to Brent Knoll across the northern Levels and you may notice an abundance of ash trees. The village of Ashcott nearby translates simply to the 'cottage by the ash'.

Join the lane and at a kink in the road take the footpath to the village. You pass through two fine eighteenth-century gateposts with the remains of a large walled garden on your left and enter a small lane to the main road.

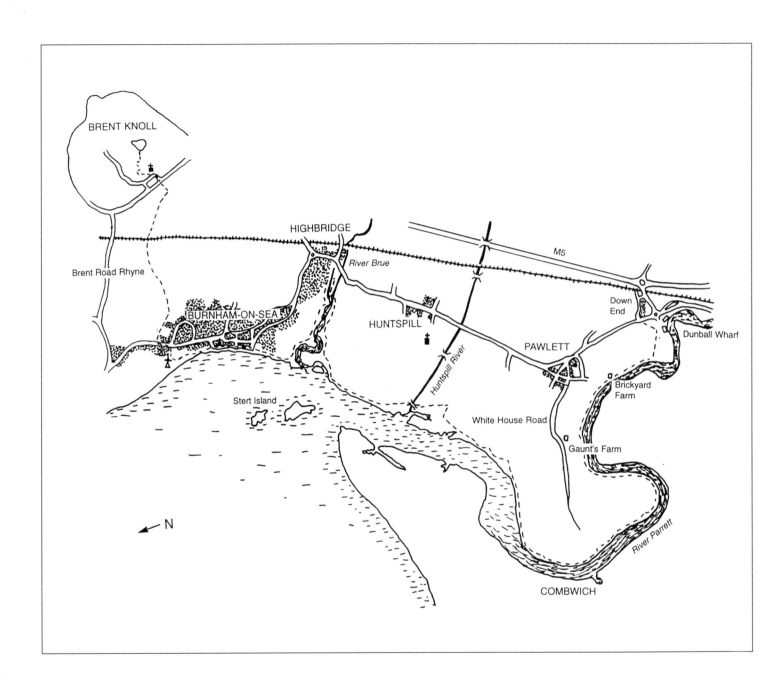

WALK SIX

Estuary, Seaside and Hill:
DUNBALL WHARF TO BRENT KNOLL
VIA BURNHAM-ON-SEA

(Pathfinder map 1217 and 1197) 16 miles.

This is the longest of the walks but the going is relatively easy and immensely enjoyable. I recommend a calm day; otherwise if a strong sea breeze is blowing from the bay you will soon tire.

There are two ways to begin the walk, the first slightly fraught because of traffic. Either park in Station Road just south of the Henry Fielding Inn and cross the split carriageway of the A38 into the wharf (there is a public right of way despite the private signs) or take the gentler option and park in Down End, crossing the A38 by the remains of the Norman keep and join the river by walking down Dunball Drove. If you do go through the wharf then take extra care. It can be busy with crane and traffic if a ship is in. The path stays next to the river after crossing the yard.

Dunball Wharf is a reminder of the Parrett's long history of marine traffic. This is the last remaining commercial wharf on the river and survives only because of the close proximity to the M5. It takes about 70 vessels a year bringing in sea-dredged sand from the Welsh side of the channel (and in 'coals to Newcastle' fashion some moss peat from Ireland for the peat industry on the Levels!).

About a mile down river from Dunball Wharf is Brickyard Farm. The row of workers' cottages built right up against the bank of the river and the flooded pits behind the modernised farm are all that is left of Pawlett's brickworks. In the nineteenth century the Bridgwater area was famous for the variety of bricks and tiles it produced, tapping into the rich source of clay within the hinterland of the river.

The village stretches out along a ridge and ahead of you is Combwich with the pylons and cables from Hinkley Point snaking across the landscape. They gain height on the river for the ships to Dunball Wharf. To the south are the distinctive hills of the Quantocks.

Along the banks of the river you will see the occasional trappings of fishermen, their ramshackle lock ups and little used kit telling the story of a dying tradition. Although the river is full of silt, salmon swim into the estuary, possibly lost on their journey to the cleaner waters of the Wye. They have been fished for centuries by both net and trap. On a low tide you can still see the lines of salmon butts stretching down the muddy banks of the river. Conical in shape, they capture the fish on the high tide, trapping them by the gills as the waters turn and leaving them high and dry.

At one time all the traps were made of withies but are now of galvanised wire. A fisherman from Stretcholt told me this poignant story which illustrates the possible death knell for the trade. Salmon catches have fallen in recent years and the cost of the licence was more than the value of his catch. Having lost heart he piled all his butts into a heap and set fire to them. 'I was damned if I was going to pay the NRA for all my hard work.'

Tied to the fences of the river-bank are small boats known as 'Bridgwater Flatners' which are used to net the river. Their broad shallow keels provide good stability and can skim over the strong tides in the estuary.

At the end of the Pawlett ridge and nestling just slightly above the flood plain is the ancient farm of Gaunt's, watched over by a giant building looming out from behind the trees. This is a remnant from the Second World War, a hangar which housed a barrage balloon to protect the Royal Ordnance factory at Puriton from aerial attack.

As you reach the bank directly opposite Combwich you will see a wide track marked on the map as White House Road winding back towards Pawlett. The road is very old and was in use by the Romans when Combwich was their main port on the Parrett. They might well have navigated to their fortified town of Ilchester by means of the Parrett and Yeo, but the ridge road across the Poldens was also an important route. The name 'White House' refers to an inn that was here at the time of the Monmouth Rebellion and fell into ruin at the end of the nineteenth century. The garden and walls can still be seen to the left of the track.

There is no record of a bridge here in Roman times and it is assumed that the crossing was by ford, remembering that the river and estuary have changed a great deal since then. Ferries were in use from the Middle Ages until this century but cross no more. The pull of the Anchor Inn on the other side will have to be ignored.

As you meander, the mouth of the river gets wider and Burnham-on-Sea comes into view. By the time you reach the 'island' the view has opened up revealing Brent Knoll in the distance, the Mendips behind, Brean Down and a mud brown sea towards Wales. Look out for shelducks which enjoy feeding along this stretch.

The coastline is forever on the move and so the river map is constantly updated. Peter Lee works as the Harbour Master and Pilot for the port of Bridgwater and guides in the ships coming up to Dunball:

> The ship masters are all expert navigators but they don't have the local knowledge of the river. The deep water channels often change and further up river, especially on a flood tide, they have been known to switch from one bank to another!

> We have to walk the river every two weeks to monitor the channels at low tide. In the ten years that I have worked here there has never been an accident with the big ships, but a yachtsman coming down from Combwich on a unusually high tide mistook a beacon for one on the Brue and sailed into a flooded field. The waters receded and the boat stayed there for a month with the cows wandering around it!

The path zigzags around the island and crosses over the Huntspill River via the clyse.

The Huntspill Cut was opened in 1942 and killed two birds with one stone. The Royal Ordnance factory built at Puriton required several million gallons of water a day and the Drainage Board of the Brue Valley saw this as an ideal opportunity to improve their drainage. Although called a river it is more like a reservoir with a pumping station at Gold Corner lifting the water in and the clyses releasing it as and when the conditions in the Parrett estuary allow.

The path now joins a made up road but the best views are gained by walking along the sea defence. The mouth of the Brue acts as a small harbour for yachts with one working trawler that fishes the bay. Like the river fishing, times aren't good and the owners of the trawler told me about their trade:

> The problem now is a bit of pollution but mainly over fishing. The fish stocks are definitely going down with the Spanish and the Dutch and everyone else hammering away at the Irish Sea. There aren't many resident fish in the bay so you're always hoping something will come up.
>
> At Hinkley Point they suck in so much water that they bring in all the young fish and shrimps, there's thousands of them going through the system. They're filtered and put into baskets but what isn't caught in the screen goes right through the cooling system. It comes out like fish soup. The mullet seem to like it but they're the only fish that do. They put in an ultrasound a couple of years back but it frightened the fish right out of the bay. They could pick the sound up in Swansea!
>
> Fishing is still a living, or part of a living anyway. It's not so good now as it used to be but we keep trying.

Walk up river and cross over on the Highbridge clyse. Turn right and follow the row of houses until you reach one with a flat roof. A small path leads down to the back of a new housing estate and turning left brings you out on the lane behind the old sawmills. You can now walk back down the Brue to Burnham.

Burnham became 'on-Sea' in 1917, a decision no doubt to encourage more holiday trade. It was once a small village surrounded by farmland but expanded in the late eighteenth century as it became fashionable to take the air and summer by the sea. Another attraction, which proved to be very short

Keith Bastow and Ron Wyatt, Fishermen, Burnham-on-Sea. 'Fishing is a living, or part of a living anyway. It's not so good now as it used to be, but we keep trying.'

lived, was the discovery of mineral springs by a local curate, who also seems to have been the town's entrepreneur. In the 1830s the Reverend David Davies built a Bath House, hoping his investment would launch the town as a spa. His enthusiasm however failed to convince the visitor whose description of the waters as sulphurous and smelly leads one to wonder at the source!

The Great Western Railway with a station at Highbridge improved Burnham's trade and in 1858 the Somerset and Dorset line came to the town, terminating with a line extending onto a pier to meet steamboat traffic from Wales. The intention was for a link from Wales with the Dorset coast and then on to France. As well as goods the holiday maker travelled this route and many people chose to stay in the town.

As you walk into town you look into the backyard of a holiday village, built in the 1960s on the site of Pillsmouth Farm. The eighteenth-century agricultural improver, Richard Locke, lived at the farm and was the driving spirit behind many of the drainage schemes for Sedgemoor. Locke was obsessed with reclamation and promised high value per acre if his schemes were implemented. There is a touch of irony in the present scene. The last farmer of Pillsmouth certainly maximised the land's potential for profit.

Burnham is now a popular town in the holiday season and is a shopping magnet for the caravan parks that stretch up the coast. The concrete esplanade, with nouveau victorian lamps and bollards, has been smartened recently; but the money spent here was not just for a facelift. On 13 December 1981 a furious storm behind a high tide sent a tidal wave up the Parrett, which swept across the farmland taking sheep, pigs, gates and every helpless being in its wake. Holes were punched in the town's sea wall and boulders and cars were bounced along the sea front. Some seven hundred houses were flooded. When you step onto the beach look at the new sea wall. It was designed with a curve to throw back the force of the waves.

Peter Lee, Harbour Master, checking the pilot light on Burnham Church tower.

The lower lighthouse, Burnham-on-Sea. Built in the nineteenth century, it was converted to a sector light in the 1960s when the inland lighthouse became redundant.

The wreck of the SS Nornen *at low tide. Looking like the bones of a whale the Norwegian barge* Nornen *came aground in a storm of 1897.*

The church of St Andrew, with its precarious leaning tower, sits down in its churchyard giving an indication of the level of the old village which at one time would have straggled behind a sea defence of wall and dune. Just below the gilded weathercock on the tower's staircase turret is a pilot lamp, used to guide ships from the Bristol Channel into the mouth of the Parrett.

This tradition began with the wife of a fisherman leaving a candle in their cottage window to guide his boat home. Other sailors then paid towards the cost and the church sexton transferred the right to the church. Reverend Davies, with an eye to an income, then built a lighthouse tower, the remains of which can be seen above the roof of the house to the left. In 1829 Trinity House bought him out and built the two lighthouses to the north of the town.

These operated as transit lights, so that when they were almost in line the ships would know to turn into the Parrett's mouth. In the 1960s the system was changed and the inland house became redundant. The lower one now has sector lights which help the ships turn from port to starboard depending on which colour they can see. They then line up with the light on the church tower and another on the sea wall.

Walk across the sandflats to the wooden lighthouse and take the small path through the sand dunes, out onto Gore Road. The inland lighthouse is rather surreal, sticking up behind the suburban houses. At the end of the road turn left and walk past the lighthouse. Flanked on either side by the keepers' lodges, the property is now divided into three. The tower was sold for conversion to a house in 1995. I envy the occupants their view but not the climb. Cross the main road and turn right into Shelley Drive. Take a right into Brambles Road and follow a path signposted on your left to Brent Broad Farm.

As you leave the suburbs of Burnham behind, the path now opens between two hedges and is bordered by a rhyne. Note on the map how it curves, indicating an earlier date than most of the straighter rhynes. This is the course of an ancient river, referred to as the Siger in Saxon times, that has long since disappeared. During the floods of 1960 an aerial photograph was taken looking west and the water-filled fields revealed the old river course as it meandered towards the sea.

Follow this path over the railway line and into Brent Knoll. Formerly South Brent (the settlement south of the hill) the village stretches along a road at the foot of the Knoll with the church of St Michael occupying a warm and pleasant setting above. Inside the church there is much to see, but the real treasures for me are the three carved bench ends in the central aisle. Somerset is rich in these but it is unusual for them to link as a story. In medieval times the power in the landscape was held by the abbey of Glastonbury and the see of Wells. The amount of land under their control and the rents they received were not always popular with the people and the carver has taken great pleasure in telling the tale.

They depict the Abbot of Glastonbury dressed as a fox, although it has been suggested that they may be more blatant and refer to Richard Fox, the Bishop of Bath and Wells. In either case he comes a cropper, first by humiliation in the stocks and finally on the gallows. The little details surrounding the event with the monks dressed as pigs, the monkey with the tithes and the fox addressing his 'flock' all add to the black humour.

Now leave the church and be punished for the bench ends by ascending the Knoll. This may seem extremely cruel after such a long walk and it is steep, but like me you have probably driven past this prominent mound hundreds of times on the motorway and never thought to climb it. I always remembered that it was somewhere near a service station, never looked natural, and was ample warning for the smell of rotten eggs at Bridgwater!

The reward on top, though, is worth the effort. A hill like this

Would-be glider pilots leaving Brent Knoll.

80

is rare and you can walk around the summit in a matter of minutes and feel as if you are lifting off. Glastonbury shows itself well to the east and to the west the view over the coast, with the Parrett shining as it meets the sea, is truly inspiring.

The hill was fortified in the Iron Age and was also occupied by the Romans and their earthworks, along with some later quarry -ing, give the hill a man-made appearance. It last served a military purpose as a look out post for the Home Guard.

The hill never developed as a religious site but was a draw for John Wesley, the founding minister of Methodism. When he visited Brent in the late eighteenth century he climbed up here. His preaching and evangelical style were popular with the farming folk but in the towns he sometimes suffered at the hands of the mob. He loved this view for the peace, deeming it to be the best in all England. I am not a deeply religious man but one of his prayers, with its simple message, perhaps found its roots on this hill and is worth repeating:

> Do all the good you can
> By all the means you can
> In all the ways you can
> In all the places you can
> At all the times you can
> To all the people you can
> As long as ever you can.

Acknowledgements

Secrets of the Levels is based on a television series made for HTV in Bristol. I would like to thank the following people and organizations for their help and support with the project:

David Parker and Available Light Productions Ltd for producing the programmes and proposing the original idea to HTV, and Phillip Priestley, John Podpadec, John Bennett and Bill Roberts for their skill and patience on location; my thanks also to English Nature, the RSPB, the Somerset Wildlife Trust, Somerset County Council and especially to Bernard Storer for his invaluable advice throughout the series.

It was as an art student that I first visited the Levels and although there have been inevitable changes, this peopled landscape is still one that I love. To name everybody that helped with the series and the book would take too long, but you know who you are and my grateful thanks to you all.

I would finally like to thank Anne and Jim Woodbourne for making Helen and me very comfortable whilst researching this book and to offer a toast to the health of dear Stanley Derham, who thought nothing of delivering five gallons of his 'self levelling' cider down to Devon in time for our wedding party!